BRITAIN IN OLD PHOTOGRAPHS

ISLINGTON

DAVID WITHEY & VADA HART

LONDON BOROUGH OF ISLINGTON
LIBRARY AND LEISURE SERVICES

ALAN SUTTON PUBLISHING LIMITED

Alan Sutton Publishing Limited
Phoenix Mill · Far Thrupp · Stroud
Gloucestershire · GL5 2BU

First published 1995

Copyright © London Borough of Islington, 1995

Cover photographs: (*front*): the construction of
Rosebery Avenue, 1891; *back*: Barnsbury Park
School, 1906.

British Library Cataloguing in Publication Data.
A catalogue record for this book is available from
the British Library.

ISBN 0-7509-1012-7

Typeset in 9/10 Sabon.
Typesetting and origination by
Alan Sutton Publishing Limited.
Printed in Great Britain by
Ebenezer Baylis, Worcester.

This book is dedicated to the many supportive
people who have, over the years, given
photographs and other material to the Islington
Local History Collections. We are grateful for
their assistance.

Hugh Myddelton School, Sans Walk, 1907.

Contents

Finsbury Park Empire Theatre, 1963. The Empire was opened as a music hall in 1910. In 1914 it showed the first all-American music hall programme in Britain, and the first all-women programme in this country too. It was closed in 1960 and demolished in 1965. Vaudeville Court flats are now on the site.

Introduction

The London Borough of Islington stretches from Hornsey Lane and Highgate Hill in the north to the edge of the City of London. Created in 1964, the new borough brought together the old boroughs of Islington and Finsbury. These dated back to 1900; before that St Mary, Islington had been a separate parish, as had both Clerkenwell and St Luke's, Finsbury. Islington and Finsbury have a shared history, which dates back to the manorial lands of the middle ages.

The period of history covered by this collection of photographs begins in the 1860s and 1870s, though most of the postcard views are from the Edwardian era. We see here a very different world from our own, roads busy with horse-buses, motor-buses, trains and the occasional new-fangled motor-car, but still safe enough for pedestrians to amble across. Children play in the streets as well as the parks. Errand boys dawdle on street corners. Working groups include the very young and the old. Buildings of a former age are still to be seen and architecture is on a human scale. (Skyward stacks of offices and flats are yet to come.) Fashions then would be outrageous now; just look at the outsize hats, the furbelows and flounces of the Edwardian ladies, the Eton-collared boys, the cabmen in bowlers and breeches.

While nostalgia has its place, some changes have been for the better. From the 1860s and 1870s much progress was made in education and public health. Overcrowded courts and rookeries were swept away, new housing built, water supplies and drainage laid on. Medical services gradually improved. New roads were constructed, such as Rosebery Avenue, built in 1889 to link Islington with the West End.

The story was not all hopeful. Islington and Finsbury suffered widespread unemployment and poverty early this century. The 1930s were lean times. The Finsbury Plan and the opening of the Finsbury Health Centre in 1938 attempted to address housing and health problems in this area. The Second World War brought widespread devastation. Post-war rebuilding changed the local landscape and improved living conditions. Few people now live in the overcrowded, insanitary surroundings which some of today's senior citizens experienced. (Many remember terrace houses without bathrooms, and a lavatory some way down the street shared with other families.)

Some of the grander streets and squares, particularly in Highbury, remained immune from decay and dereliction, but there was much social and environmental decline. The 'gentrification' of areas like Barnsbury in the 1960s and 1970s has put the process in reverse, and urban renewal is now the order of the day.

This book takes us on a journey through Islington's past, by horse-bus, cab and tram, passing by elegant department stores, sturdy terraces and stout squares, through jostling crowds in the markets, past workaday factories and grim backstreets. Here we have the Islington of yesteryear, sometimes quite recognizable, sometimes unfamiliar, but in a time of rapid change, it is all the more interesting to look at what has gone before. The photographic record is not complete, and certainly reflects and is limited by the vision of the photographers and the market for their work. Nevertheless, it forms a fascinating record of things past, and perhaps most importantly captures on camera the long-lost faces of Islington children and Islington people.

Authors' Note

We owe our picture of Islington past to the preservation of many hundreds of postcards and photographs in the Islington Local History Collections. We are grateful to all who have contributed, in whatever way, to the collections.

Thanks are also due to Doreen Freer for her untiring help and patience. Without her we could not have written this book.

ARCHWAY TO THE NAG'S HEAD

The Highgate Toll Gate, 1860s. The toll started in about 1813, when charges were 4d.

for a horse and 1d. per foot passenger, and continued until 1876. The toll gates were

removed in 1864. In the background is the original brick archway, demolished in 1895.

The old Archway Bridge, *c.* 1898. The original Highgate Archway was designed by John Nash and the foundation stone laid in 1812. It was demolished in 1898–9 and replaced by a new bridge, which was opened in 1900.

The Highgate Archway, *c.* 1904. This photograph shows the new bridge, designed by Alexander Binnie and opened on 28 July 1900.

The Archway Tavern, *c.* 1912, showing the tram terminus and workmen repairing the tramway in Archway Road. On the left are trams and buses coming down Highgate Hill. The building on the right is Archway Road Wesleyan Methodist Chapel.

The Archway Tavern, 1 Archway Road, 1904. The Tavern was rebuilt in 1886. Entertainments here included 1*s*. 3*d*. lunches, afternoon teas, evening concerts, billiards and pool. The Archway Tavern was the terminus for buses to and from Victoria, as well as being the tram terminus for services from King's Cross, Euston and Moorgate.

Junction Road, *c.* 1906. Junction Road was laid in 1811 to link Kentish Town and Holloway Road. It was developed as a residential area in the 1850s. This view shows the Archway end, with the original Archway Road Wesleyan Methodist Chapel (replaced by Archway Central Hall) in the background.

The Whittington Stone public house and Whittington Stone (on the corner of the street), Highgate Hill, *c.* 1906. The stone where Dick Whittington was said to have rested was originally part of a wayside cross where poor lepers came to collect food and alms. It was broken up in 1795 and replaced several times before the present stone, made in 1854 and repaired in 1935, was erected at the corner of Salisbury Walk and Highgate Hill. The stone was later moved near the corner of Magdala Avenue. The figure of a cat was added in 1964. The public house dates from about 1860.

The Boston Hotel, Junction Road, 1904. This public house was first opened as the Boston Arms Tavern in 1860. It was rebuilt in 1899. It was burned out in 1967 and reopened in 1968.

Tufnell Park Road, *c.* 1900. Tufnell Park Road was started in the 1820s and built up by the 1870s. St George's Church, on the right, based on a Crusader round building, was designed by George Trufitt in 1867. It was replaced by a new church in 1975. The old building has been converted into the St George's Theatre.

GPO, Manor Gardens, *c.* 1912. This was originally the Post Office Money Order Department and later became the GPO Training Centre. From 1986 to 1994 it was used as offices. The building is now called the Beaux Arts Building and has been converted into flats.

The Archway Tavern, Highgate.

Archway junction, *c.* 1912, showing the Archway Tavern and, in the foreground (centre), Archway Road Wesleyan Methodist Chapel, designed by John Johnston and built in 1872–3 by Dove Brothers. The chapel advertises 'temperance entertainment

Junction of Holloway Road and Marlborough Road, Upper Holloway, *c.* 1905. In the centre is the Nag's Head and on the right the Marlborough Theatre.

every Tuesday'. The building had become delapidated by the 1920s and was replaced by
Archway Central Hall.

The Nag's Head, Holloway Road, April 1898. This public house has been in existence since the 1850s and has gradually become a local landmark. The covered wagon and horse-bus are passing Abbot's boot and shoe shop.

A horse-bus stands near Lipton's, tea and provision merchant, Seven Sisters Road, c. 1906. Next door to Lipton's were Charles Baker, tailors, and Richard Bridgeland, mantle makers.

Residents (possibly the Farleys) of 26 Thane Villas, Holloway, 1910.

The gates of Finsbury Park, Seven Sisters Road, *c.* 1906. This view was taken near the old tramway depot. The Rink Cinema, with a skating rink to the rear, was opened on the site in 1909. In 1923 it showed the first 'talking picture' in Britain. It was closed in 1958.

Section Two

LOWER HOLLOWAY TO HIGHBURY

The Northern Polytechnic, Holloway Road, c. 1906. This is now part of North London University. It was built by Charles Bell in 1896 on the site of Osnaburgh Cottages, and was extended by A.W. Cooksey in 1902.

Holloway Road, 1905, looking towards the Nag's Head. The cab rank is outside Hart's furnishers, and the horse-bus is passing James Selby, linen drapers.

Drayton Park, *c.* 1912. The photograph shows delivery boys in the foreground and a lamplighter working on a streetlamp in the background. Drayton Park was commenced in 1841 as Highbury Hill Park and built up during the period 1855–65. By the 1870s it was known as Drayton Park.

Gardens behind St Mary Magdalene's Church, Holloway Road, *c.* 1906. St Mary Magdalene was opened in 1814 as a chapel of ease to St Mary's Islington. It became a separate parish in 1894. The burial ground was cleared in 1894 and became a public garden.

Highbury Corner and station, 1920. On the left is the ornate station building and on the right Barclays Bank. Nowadays it would be unwise to saunter across Holloway Road as the pedestrians are doing here.

Highbury Place, *c.* 1906, showing a London General horse-bus on the Angel route. Highbury Place was built in the 1770s in the fields to the north of Islington. In Edwardian times this was the area in which to find a doctor or dentist.

Calabria Road, Highbury, *c*. 1906. Calabria Road dates from 1890. Richard Thomas Baines, a well-known theatre journalist of the day, lived at No. 73 from 1895 to 1899.

Shops in Highbury Place, *c*. 1912. The photograph shows Mrs Edith Lockwood's milliners shop, and a little girl with a skipping rope outside Thomas Grant, fruiterer. Next door is Arthur Bellew's builder's yard.

A game of tennis in Highbury Fields, *c.* 1912. Highbury Fields was opened to the public in 1885 and enlarged in 1891.

Children walking in Highbury Fields, *c.* 1919. The children on the right, taking the air with grandmother, are very well presented, while the group on the left appear more rough and ready.

Highbury Hill House, *c*. 1912. Built in about 1719 to the design of D.A. Alexander, architect of Dartmoor Prison, for Dr William Saunders, physician at Guy's Hospital, the house became a school in 1894 (a training college and kindergarten of the Home and Colonial School Society). In 1912 the London County Council took this over as a girls' secondary school. The old house was replaced by a new building in 1928; the school became Highbury Fields School in 1981.

The Highbury Clock Tower, *c.* 1900. The clock tower stands opposite Christ Church, Highbury Grove. Made of cast iron, it was presented to Islington Vestry in 1897 by Alfred Hutchinson of 62 Highbury Park to commemorate Queen Victoria's diamond jubilee. New dials were fitted in 1959.

The Highbury Barn public house at the corner of Highbury Grove and Kelvin Road, *c.* 1906. The No. 19 bus stopped here. Originally a farm building, the Highbury Barn became a pleasure resort in the eighteenth century and by the 1860s was a grand venue where the famous Leotard did his athletic exercises and Blondin his high-wire act. The gardens were closed in 1872.

Highbury Park, *c.* 1906. Development of the road began between 1812 and 1815. Edwardian Highbury Park was the home of several clinics, a doctor or two and numerous shopkeepers.

The Broadway, Highbury Park, *c.* 1906. The rather grand shops were built in 1895. The Ten Per Cent Wine Co. was at No. 1, on the right, next door to Scrase & Sons, bootmakers, Harry Leonard, tailor, and Samuel Puttnam, oilman.

Highbury Park Tavern public house, Highbury Quadrant, *c.* 1925. Highbury Quadrant was built up in the 1870s.

Highbury New Park, *c.* 1906. Highbury New Park was developed by Henry Rydon in the 1850s. The residents were given permission to plant trees on either side at their own expense in 1875.

NEWINGTON GREEN

TO

ISLINGTON GREEN

Petherton Road, 1906. This road was built up in the 1870s on land owned by Henry

Rydon. The Highbury Microscopical and Scientific Society met at 80 Petherton Road from

1888 to 1893. The road was badly damaged by bombs during the Second World War.

Newington Green, *c.* 1906. Newington Green was already in existence in the fifteenth century. It remained rural up to the late eighteenth century. Railings were first added in 1742. Many nonconformist clergy settled here in the seventeenth and eighteenth centuries. Mary Wollstonecraft (1759–97), the mother of Mary Shelley, ran a school here with her sister Eliza from 1784 to 1786.

Newington Green, looking towards Elmes & Co., exhibition fitters, Albion Road (Hackney), *c.* 1924.

Islington Green, 1906. Nannies and their charges are taking the air.

Mildmay Park, *c.* 1906. Mildmay Park was built in the early 1850s on land owned by the Mildmay family.

Jay's, watchmakers, Essex Road, *c*. 1910. The villas on the right have been replaced by the Marquess Estate.

Essex Road, *c*. 1910. Essex Road Station, on the right, dates from 1904. The Three Brewers public house on the opposite side of the road dates back to 1832 and was a tied house of the Cannon Brewery.

The Essex Road Bakery and the King's Head public house. The original King's Head dates from 1805.

Upper Street and Islington Green, 1904. The horses are drinking at the trough near the corner of Essex Road.

Statue of Sir Hugh Myddelton, Islington Green, *c*. 1864. The statue, by John Thomas, commemorates the seventeenth-century entrepreneur of the New River. It was funded jointly by Sir Morton Peto, The New River Company and the people of Islington, and unveiled by Gladstone on 2 August 1862. This picture was used as a trade card for the photographer J.F. Hasset, who had premises at 62 Upper Street from 1864 to 1871.

HIGHBURY CORNER
TO THE ANGEL

St Paul's Road, c. 1906. St Paul's Road was mainly developed during the period
1840–63. It was originally Hopping Lane, an ancient roadway leading from Highbury
to Ball's Pond.

Compton Terrace, *c.* 1905. The terrace was begun by Henry Leroux between 1806 and 1810. The five houses at the end near Highbury Corner were damaged by a V2 rocket attack on 27 June 1944 and subsequently demolished.

Canonbury Park North, *c.* 1906. This was a street of Victorian villas. Mrs Mary Vivian Hughes, author of the family saga *A London Family 1870–1900*, lived at 1 Canonbury Park North, which was demolished in 1937.

The New River, Douglas Road, Canonbury, *c.* 1906. Douglas Road was built in 1850. It is now part of the Marquess Estate. The New River was a water channel projected by Sir Hugh Myddelton in the early seventeenth century to bring water from springs at Amwell and Chadwell, in Hertfordshire, to New River Head.

The New River, near Douglas Road, *c.* 1906. Until 1946 about half a mile of the New River remained as open water. This stretch is now New River Walk. The water channel was reconstructed in the 1970s.

Willow Bridge Road from Canonbury Place, *c.* 1905. The road took its name from the nearby Willow Bridge, which crosses the New River.

Canonbury Square, *c.* 1920. Built by Henry Leroux, the square was first occupied in 1826. Famous residents include Samuel Phelps, George Orwell, Evelyn Waugh, Duncan Grant and Vanessa Bell.

A decorated cart representing British Justice, Islington Carnival, June 1900.

Upper Street, from Highbury Corner, 1905. On the left is the Union Chapel and on the right the Old Cock Tavern. The original tavern was there in 1780. In 1872 it was rebuilt as part of Highbury station. Damaged during the Second World War, it was rebuilt again, this time adjacent to the new station.

Upper Street, *c.* 1900. On the left, near the corner of Park Street, is Rackstraw's Drapery Stores, Nos 208–15, and on the right Compton Terrace.

Upper Street, looking down towards St Mary's Church from the fire station, *c.* 1912. A group of mothers and children is passing No. 150, the International Glove Co., while the Highbury station tram is followed by a motor-bus.

A float representing T.R. Roberts' department store, Upper Street, outside the shop, Islington Carnival, *c.* 1904.

St Mary's Islington, 1907. A church existed on this site in the Middle Ages. It was replaced by a building with a low tower in about 1483. This was rebuilt in 1754 by Lancelot Dowbiggin. The church was bombed in 1940 and rebuilt in 1956.

Upper Street, Islington, looking north, *c*. 1906. The spire belongs to Unity Church, which is next door to the fire station. It was badly damaged by bombing in 1940 and rebuilt in 1958. The police station and the Vestry Hall are to the left of the church.

A surprisingly tranquil view of Upper Street, from Islington Green, 1906. The Fox public house is advertising BOVRIL in lights.

The Upper Street frontage of the Royal Agricultural Hall, *c.* 1898. The building was opened in 1862 as a centre for the Smithfield Club's cattle shows. It was a main exhibition venue for Victorian London, with horse shows, Crufts Dog Shows, revivalist meetings and circuses among the many events held there.

Collins' Music Hall, Islington Green, 1906. The music hall was started in the Lansdowne Arms public house in 1863 by Sam Collins Vagg, the Irish entertainer. Rebuilt in 1897, it featured stars like Kate Carney, Charlie Chaplin (1912), Gracie Fields (1915), Marie Lloyd and George Robey. It was closed after a fire in 1958, and later became part of the former Andersons timber business.

Colebrooke Row, *c.* 1916. Colebrooke Row was built between 1768 and 1771 on land belonging to the Colebrooke family, important local landowners. No. 32a Colebrooke Row was the home of William Woodfall (1746–1803), a pioneer of Hansard and parliamentary reporting. It was demolished in 1952 and Hermitage House was built on the site.

Duncan Terrace, *c.* 1916. Duncan Terrace was built in 1791 and was named after Admiral Adam Duncan (1731–1804), who had defeated the Dutch in the war against Holland and France in the 1790s.

Colebrooke Row, *c.* 1916, showing Charles George Goord's Colebrooke Works. Goord made fancy leather goods, inkstands and jewel boxes and had offices and showrooms in City Road.

Upper Street, looking north, with open-top buses and horse-drawn traffic during the 1920s. On the left, behind the tram stop, is 1 Upper Street, a pawnbroker's shop owned by Sidney Smith, Honorary Secretary of the National Pawnbrokers' Association.

Liverpool Road, *c.* 1906. On the left is the Prince Regent public house at the corner of Richmond Road. On the right are Peter Ebert's bakery, at No. 126, Edwin Booth, grocer, and Frank Turner, signwriter.

Girls of Islington Drill Brigade in North Road, Islington Carnival, 19 September 1907.

Pierrots at the Caledonian Market, Islington Carnival, 19 September 1907.

Caledonian Road, *c.* 1905. The cattle are being driven towards the Caledonian Market from the Great Northern Railway Cattle Depot. The church behind is the Wesleyan Methodist Chapel, Hillmarton Road, which closed in 1915. It became St Mary's Liberal Catholic Church for the period 1926–76 and was demolished in 1980.

The Great Northern fish and chip shop, 124 York Road, 1903. The window poster advertises Buffalo Bill's Show at Olympia. Patrons could follow fish and chips with chocolates or tobacco from the shop next door or a drink at the City of York on the other side.

CLERKENWELL AND SOUTH OF THE ANGEL

Vernon Square, c. 1906, one of Clerkenwell's fine squares. This view is enlivened by the obvious curiosity of the children.

The Angel, as seen in *Punch*, 1889. The scene is dominated by the Angel Hotel, which was built on the site of the original Angel Inn, which gave the locality its name.

The Angel, 1900.

The Blue Coat Boy public house, City Road, *c.* 1916. The original public house is said to have been built in 1636. The sign was originally above the door and shows a boy in charity school uniform. This building was demolished during the redevelopment of the Angel in the late 1980s.

The construction of Rosebery Avenue, showing Sadlers Wells Theatre and, in the distance, the Clown public house in St John Street, 1891. The steam-driven crane in the background is mounted on rails.

The construction of the second section of Rosebery Avenue. This section ran between Garnault Place and St John Street, and was opened in December 1891. The photograph shows the central service chambers, still visible today between Sadlers Wells Theatre on the left and Spa Green on the right. Opposite Sadlers Wells, immediately behind the crane-bucket, stood Deacon's Music Hall. It was demolished to accommodate the new road a few months before this photograph was taken.

The official opening by Lord Rosebery of the first section of Rosebery Avenue, between Grays Inn Road and Farringdon Road, 21 July 1890. Mr Irons, Surveyor to Clerkenwell Vestry, is standing in the centre. The Clerkenwell Fire Station, on the right, provided two hand-propelled fire ladders to support the flags across the new road, and local bus drivers wore Lord Rosebery's racing colours for the day.

Myddelton Street, off St John Street, showing the busy intersection with Garnault Place, Skinner Street and Exmouth Market. This scene, photographed in the early years of the century, shows buildings which are all now demolished with the exception of Clerkenwell Vestry Hall, on the extreme left of the view.

Coronation party in Lloyd's Row, off St John Street, 1937.

Lloyd's Row, off St John Street, 1937. In the centre stands the last building to house the Islington Spa, or New Tunbridge Wells. Dating from 1685, the minerally enriched spring discovered on this site was to rival and surpass its neighbour, Sadlers Wells. The spa was frequented by nobility and royalty, who came to take of the waters, which were claimed to cure so much and were sufficiently distasteful to convince many. To distract the throngs, the site had been laid out with walks, arbours, lime trees, a dancing room, raffling shop, other gambling rooms and a coffee shop. It was all to decline in popularity and profitability in the early nineteenth century. By the 1840s the whole complex had contracted into this one building, which housed the original water source in a basement cupboard. In the 1890s it dried up completely. The Islington Spa building and the rest of Lloyd's Row were demolished to make way for Spa Green Estate (1948) and the Hugh Myddelton Primary School.

Northampton Institute, St John Street, 1906. The institute was built on the site of the manor-house of Clerkenwell, which was presented by the Marquis of Northampton in 1896. It was built at a cost of £50,000 and opened in 1898, originally as a branch of the City Polytechnic. It became independent when the polytechnic was dissolved in 1907. In 1957 the Northampton Institute was designated a College of Advanced Technology. It was incorporated by Royal Charter as a university on 23 May 1966 and renamed the City University.

In spite of the distinctive red-brick, with facings and finishings of stone, and its dome-capped central tower, the building was dwarfed by its neighbour, Smithfield Martyr's Memorial Church (St Peter's), which was built in 1869–71. The site was again a gift from the Marquis of Northampton. The church served as a memorial to the Reformers who suffered for their faith in Smithfield, and its site was the nearest obtainable to the scene of their martyrdom. The building was in the French Gothic style and bore reliefs of the martyrs in whose memory it had been erected. The church was seriously damaged during the Second World War and finally demolished in 1956.

Clerkenwell Green, 1946–7. This photograph shows the typical light-industrial businesses, so common in Clerkenwell, sharing premises with residents on upper floors. A further insight into the development of Clerkenwell is embodied in the Marx Memorial Library, located across the green from these buildings.

The distressed details of an earlier age at Clerkenwell Green, 1978.

Newcastle Place, off Clerkenwell Close, 1974. Newcastle Place was built in 1794 by James Carr, the architect of St James' Church.

Clerkenwell Green, c. 1898. The children are drinking from the Good Samaritan Temperance Society fountain, which had been set up in 1862 by public subscription. In 1872 it had been the focal point of a large public meeting at which Archbishop Manning had administered the temperance pledge.

Italian ice-cream seller, Clerkenwell Green, July 1900. Whatever has attracted the attention of the group of men is unknown, but it is certainly not ice-cream. The railings behind surround the churchyard of St James' Church, Clerkenwell Close.

St John's Square, c. 1902. Members of the Order of St John of Jerusalem are crossing the square between St John's Gate and St John's Church. The modern Order of St John re-acquired St John's Gate as its headquarters in 1874.

A visit by King Edward VII to St John's Church, St John's Square, *c*. 1902.

Percy Circus, Great Percy Street, showing the fine, large houses erected in the 1840s. In 1905, the date this photograph was taken, the occupants of 16 Percy Circus included Vladimir and Krupskaya Lenin.

Holford Square, *c*. 1905. Lenin, the architect of the Russian Revolution in 1917 and founder of the Soviet Union, lived in the first floor flat of 30 Holford Square between April 1902 and April 1903. The landlady of the home knew her lodger as 'Mr Richter' and assumed that he was German. It was this name which he used to obtain a reading ticket at the British Museum Library, where he spent much of his time. In her memoirs, his wife, Krupskaya, recalls: 'Ilych studied living London. He loved going on long rides about the town on top of an omnibus. He liked the movement of this huge commercial city. The quiet squares, the detached houses, with their separate entrances and shining windows adorned with greenery.'

However, Lenin's fascination with London was not that of a tourist: 'But tucked away nearby, the mean little streets, inhabited by the London working people, where lines with washing hung across the street, and pale children played in the gutter – these sights could not be seen from the bus-top.'

Lenin and Krupskaya left London for Geneva in April 1903. Holford Square was seriously damaged by bombing during the Second World War; the house associated with Lenin was destroyed.

Rowton House, King's Cross Road, was one of Lord Rowton's Victorian hotels for working men, the first of which was built in Vauxhall in 1892 at Lord Rowton's own expense. The King's Cross Rowton House was erected in 1894 by Rowton Homes Ltd which pursued a housing policy of 'philanthropy at five per cent'. By the late 1930s Rowton House still provided decent housing for working men at a reasonable charge. In 1961 the building was converted into the Mount Pleasant Hotel, where each room consisted of what had been two and a half cubicles in the working man's hotel. It was finally demolished in 1989 and replaced with the Holiday Inn Hotel.

Gwynne Place (Riceyman Steps), *c*. 1920. This unusual feature connecting King's Cross Road with Granville Square was made famous by Arnold Bennett's novel *Riceyman Steps* (1923). The local population have seen fit to refer to the location as 'Plum-Pudding Steps'. St Philip's Church, in the middle of Granville Square, was demolished in 1935.

Coronation celebrations in Affleck Street, off Pentonville Road, 1953.

Section Six

ROAD AND RAIL

The Stoke Newington to Victoria London General Omnibus Company 'Favorite' horse-bus,

c. 1900. The route ran via Charing Cross, The Strand and Essex Road.

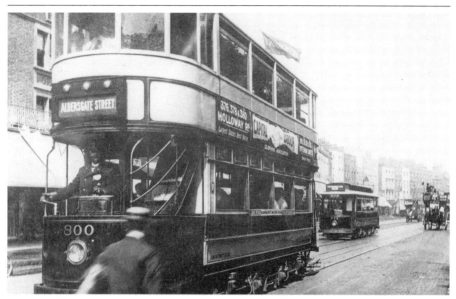

Trams and horse-buses in Upper Street, *c.* 1906. The introduction of electric trams and motor-buses early in the century spelled the end for horse-drawn public transport.

Trams in Holloway Road, at the corner of Seven Sisters Road, 1930s. An elegant young woman is about to board the Waltham Cross tram outside Abbot Shoes, while a policeman stands on traffic duty.

Horse-bus in Holloway Road, *c.* 1906.

The Finsbury Park to Peckham horse-bus outside Warman's Estate Agents, Highbury Corner, *c.* 1900. The bus is advertising Pears soap, St Julien tobacco and Carter's Little Liver Pills.

Horse vans assembled in King Square, Clerkenwell, as part of the Easter Parade in 1947. (Photograph courtesy of C. Ellmers)

Cabs and cabmen outside Canonbury station, *c.* 1900. In the background is a mail wagon, and on the right the premises of Percy Smith, estate agent, and Eastman's, cleaners and dyers.

Highbury station and Holloway Road, *c*. 1910. The Victorian station was built in 1872 to replace the old wooden station opened at Highbury Corner in 1849. The building was severely damaged by a flying bomb on 27 June 1944. The station was renovated in 1953 and rebuilt in 1968 when the Victoria Line opened.

Canonbury station, *c*. 1910. Canonbury station was opened 1 December 1870, replacing Newington and Balls Pond Road station (opened 1858). The North London Railway was built to carry commuters from north London to the City, terminating at Broad Street station.

The first tramcar at the Archway Tavern, 1872. The route ran from Moorgate via the Angel and terminated here. The 1870s saw a widespread increase in tramways both in London and other cities.

Pentonville Hill, *c.* 1906. A tram climbs the hill towards the Angel following the route of London's first omnibus, in 1829, along Pentonville Road to the bank.

London General Omnibus Company horse-bus at Highbury, *c.* 1875. This small bus ran between Highbury station and Highbury Hill. The 'Favorite' horse-bus service to Highbury was started in the 1830s and taken over in 1856 by the LGOC. Note the advertisement on the side of the house on the right for houses to be sold or let in Highbury Park.

Traffic in Upper Street, 1930s. This view is from the high pavement looking towards the Angel. Notice the Tri-pedal iron road surface.

Section Seven

BUYING AND SELLING

Shops at 253–5 Junction Road, 1904. On the left is William Scott, ironmonger and
sanitary engineer, with a fine array of tools and hardware. On the right is E.F. Phillips,
off-licence, grocers and post office.

J. Feloi's Italian Restaurant, 6 Archway Road, 1904. Two waiters stand in the doorway, between the boards advertising '1/- Ordinary' lunches, including joint, entrée, two veg., bread and cheese or sweet.

Hall & Son's tobacconists, 8 Archway Road, next to Feloi's Restaurant, 1904. A shilling would buy five Mexican cigars.

W. Huggins, barber's shop, 12
Archway Road, 1904, round
the corner from Mackintosh's
forge. The window is full of
shaving tackle, razor straps and
hair switches. The photographic
shop next door also stocks
records and horn gramophones.

H.G. Payne and Co., 29
Junction Road, 1904. This was
the place to buy Perfect Tea,
'matchless – so luscious and
pure', and 'Choicest French
Coffee as used in Paris'. Next
door is J. Pitts, butcher.

H.W. Mead, confectioner, 254 New North Road, *c.* 1914. The lady on the doorstep is Mrs Adams. Nearby was the Victoria Cinema, opened in 1912 and closed in 1957.

This postcard, published by Knowlman Bros., haberdashers, 685–9 Holloway Road, is advertising their Christmas Bazaar, 1905. It was sent to one of their customers, Mrs Griffiths, of East Finchley.

Beale's Restaurant, Holloway Road, 1893. Beale's was a very grand Victorian Gothic bakery and restaurant, designed by F. Wallen, with splendid banqueting rooms and stained glass windows. It was demolished in 1970. Beale's Bakery opened at South Place, Tibberton Square, in 1829 and moved to Holloway Road in 1866. New premises were built in 1889.

Beale's Restaurant, seen from Camden Road, *c*. 1969. The building opposite is Jones Bros. Department Store, which started in 1870 at Peartree Terrace, Holloway Road, and had become a large department store by 1905.

Jones Bros., Holloway Road, as a fashionable department store, *c*. 1905.

Jacobs, kosher butcher,
24 Liverpool Road (Chapel
Market). From the Edwardian
period, this business served the
local Jewish community. The
local synagogue in Lofting Road
was closed in 1958 because the
congregation had dwindled as a
result of migration further north,
and the shop closed in the 1980s.

H. Briggs, cigar and tobacco store, 50 Newington Green, *c.* 1916.

V.F.A. Cook (Oil and Colorman), 287 Goswell Road, *c.* 1908. The premises were occupied by Victor Frederick Cook and family between approximately 1897 and 1908. Mr Cook worked as a skilled sheet metal worker; the shop was run by his wife, Emily, and daughters, Emily and Loretta. Apart from ironmongery and hardware the shop also sold foodstuffs including tea, jam and pickles. Victor Frederick Cook is shown standing outside the shop with his son, Frederick Victor. The family moved to Isledon Road where they resided until the 1960s. The shop was demolished by 1914, and a factory was built on the site in the 1920s.

The Temple of the Muses (Lackington, Allen & Co., Finsbury Square). Opened by the bookseller James Lackington (1746–1815), the Temple of the Muses was one of the sights of London, with its 140 foot frontage. The interior was so spacious that a stage-coach drawn by six horses could be driven around its central counter. Half-a-million books were constantly available for sale. As a Methodist, James Lackington had derived financial assistance to start his business from John Wesley, and this in spite of Wesley's assertion, that he 'could never keep a bookseller six months in his flock'. The great success of Lackington's business operation was in selling unpopular books cheaply; prior to this, unsold books were simply destroyed by booksellers and publishers. James Lackington began the trade in what is described today as 'remaindered' books. The Temple of the Muses was eventually destroyed by fire.

Trader with a donkey and cart at the Metropolitan Cattle Market (Caledonian Market), in the 1890s. Livestock were sold here on Mondays and Thursdays and there was a general market on Fridays attended by costermongers and other traders. The market closed on the outbreak of the Second World War.

Caledonian Road, c. 1904, showing Williams Bros. oil shop on the corner of Market Street, near the entrance to Pentonville Prison. Williams Bros. Direct Supply Co. had an extensive London Business selling groceries and other domestic supplies.

The Clock Tower and market buildings, Caledonian Market, 1962. This view shows the market buildings prior to demolition in about 1967. The Market Estate was built on the site. The Clock Tower remains as a focal point. The original structure was built in 1854/5 and was one of London's largest turret clocks. Bombed in 1940, it has undergone several restorations.

Street market in Essex Road, 1907. Passing trams must have been a hazard to stallholders and shoppers.

Chapel Street Market, 1911. Complaints received by Clerkenwell Vestry from local shopkeepers suggest that butchers had been 'selling on the stones' as early as 1868 in Chapel Street. It was as late as 1936 that the street was officially designated as 'Chapel Market'. Local residents remember that the market was noted for cheap food – chops and steak were 5*d*. pound, breasts of mutton 2½*d*. each, and on Sunday mornings meat was even cheaper since there were no refrigerators in which to preserve it and it had to be sold off. Dinners in the market were 1½*d*. for stewed eels and mash, or 2½*d*. for fish and chips. A boy's suit could be bought for 7*s*. 11*d*., with a pair of boots for 2*s*. 11*d*.

Robert Brastock and family's stall on Chapel Street Market, *c*. 1900.

The local populace scan the stalls of secondhand books, manuscripts and engravings at Farringdon Road Book Market, which was in keeping with the strong association of Farringdon with printing and publishing. First introduced to Farringdon Road by George Jeffery in 1909, the stalls had been an extension of the old Fleet Market. The five barrows of books were conveyed from a bookstore in the shadow of St James' Church, Clerkenwell, to Farringdon Road. From 1947 George Jeffery was assisted by his son, George, who continued with the stalls until his retirement in 1994. This popular attraction has now disappeared.

Whitecross Street Market, *c.* 1914, showing the Old Street end of the market, with St Luke's Church in the background.

Whitecross Street Market, *c.* 1914. The earliest reference to this market is in 1861, when it is described as having over 100 costermongers. By the 1930s it sold less in the way of foodstuffs but more cosmetics, stockings and fancy goods. Unusually for London street markets, the stallholders were mostly women.

Whitecross Street Market, at the corner of Errol Street, *c.* 1900. The produce on offer seems to reflect the comparative poverty of the area.

Exmouth Market, *c.* 1906. It is evident that an unofficial market existed here in the late 1830s from local petitions, dated 1837–9, by fruiterers and greengrocers in Exmouth and Rosoman Streets against people selling from pavements. With the opening of Rosebery Avenue in July 1892 traffic was diverted from Exmouth Street to Rosebery Avenue, allowing costermongers to have freer use of the street and giving Exmouth Market legal recognition.

ISLINGTON
AT HOME

Nos 4 and 5 Rufford Street, c. 1900. This street
was situated in the 'Belle Isle' area off York Way,
which was the site of Randell's tile kilns and a
variety of 'noxious trades', from varnish-making to
horse slaughter and piggeries, which polluted the
local environment.

Pump Court, off White Horse Alley, Benjamin Street, 1925–6. Pump Court consisted of a cul-de-sac of nine houses. Each house had three rooms with the exception of one of five rooms. From front to back, the houses at one point are as little as 10 feet deep. At the time of this photograph Pump Court had eighty-four inhabitants.

Pump Court, leading into White Horse Alley. At its widest the court measured 15 feet and at its narrowest, just 5 feet.

Pump Court, showing the wash-house in No. 9 (above), which served all the tenants of the court, and the water container outside No. 9 (below), which supplied all the houses.

Nos 8–14 Fletcher Row, off Northampton Road, Clerkenwell, 1934. This corner of Clerkenwell clearly demonstrates the concentration of buildings typical in the area. Built in 1781, Fletcher Row consisted of 12 houses occupied by 117 people (1929). Like many other domestic buildings it was finally demolished to provide commercial/industrial space.

Howard's Place, off Northampton Road, Clerkenwell, 1934.

Caroline Place, Baker's Row, off Farringdon Road, 1900. This cul-de-sac between No. 7 and No. 8 Baker's Row was entered through a covered passage 3 to 4 feet wide. There were four houses, and each had two rooms with no back ventilation. Sanitary conveniences were located near the entrance to the court and were for the use of all inhabitants; they ventilated into the court. The water supply was also common to the four houses. Being a cul-de-sac with a narrow entrance, through-ventilation of the court was not possible. There were twenty-two inhabitants. Each of the houses was partly used for the manufacture of ice-cream.

The building of Ring Cross Estate, *c.* 1932, showing Radford House, partly completed, and cottages in Eden Grove. Ring Cross Estate was built by the LCC, and covered part of Georges Road, James Street, Charlotte Place, Britton Street, Hope Place and Milton Place.

15·5·33. Nº 5.

The rear of the houses between Bastwick and Gee Street, between Goswell Road and Central Street, 1933. Bastwick Street had 45 inhabited houses, occupied by 165 families in 1929. Each room averaged 2.44 people. According to the Medical Officer of Health: 'Bastwick Street may be described as a slum street, with a public house at one end, and with a public house and a catsmeat shop at the other end. It is inhabited by some of the roughest, most destructive and some of the poorest people in the borough.' He further reported that: 'A few of the houses have wireless installations; in one instance the "aerial" was formed by the wire netting of bedstead and the "earth" was soldered on to the water service pipe'. Note the wire-netted bedstead (or aerial?) relegated to the backyard in this photograph.

Hope Street, Holloway, before demolition in 1931–4. Prior to demolition the houses were damp and decaying, with damaged roofs and no sanitation. The site was used for Ring Cross School.

Hope Street, Holloway, c. 1931. These cottages were demolished by the LCC at the request of Islington council, who classed them as insanitary dwellings. In the 1930s there was much poverty and social distress in Islington.

Church Lane, looking towards Essex Road, 1934. This was an insanitary, dilapidated street demolished under the Church Lane Clearance Order 1934. The street later became St Mary's Path. Salisbury House was built on the site, and opened by the Duke of Kent in 1937. Church Cottage on St Mary's Path is the earliest building in this area. It was once the Sexton's House, shown on a map of 1735.

ISLINGTON

AT WORK

Draft horse and horse-keeper, Venables & Co.,

187–9 Essex Road, c. 1890. Venables, famous

as piano makers, had premises here from about

1866 to 1936.

A metal foundry in St John's Square, *c.* 1920.

A.T. Oliver, gold and silver watchcase makers, 25 Spencer Street, Clerkenwell, 1970. This photograph offers an insight into one of the many activities which make up the Clerkenwell watch and clock industry. (Photograph courtesy of C. Ellmers)

Atkins' Cigar Factory, York Road (off City Road). This factory was part of the Imperial Tobacco Company. These views date from the early years of this century and clearly show the segregation, by means of a partition, of men and women in the workplace.

Atkins' Cigar Factory, York (later Dingley) Road.

H.W. Fincham photographed these women workers enjoying a break on a Finsbury rooftop, *c*. 1900.

C. Pollard, scale makers, 132–4 York Road, 1903. This firm had premises here from the 1880s until 1947. York Road was an industrial area by the mid-nineteenth century; by 1903 there were a large number of factories and metalworks, as well as the small workshops making clocks, watches and balances. York Road is now York Way.

Blacksmith's forge, 225 Ball's Pond Road, 1966. The forge was in operation from 1888 to 1966, and demolished in 1967 or 1968. The business was owned first by Francis Banning and later by William Turner. In 1900 there were at least seven stables in Balls Road; and business was brisk up to the 1930s.

The blacksmith at his anvil, 225 Ball's Pond Road, September 1966. This photograph was taken by Mayor Robert Whyte, just before the forge closed.

Carts and a cab in Brewis Brothers' Yard, Rufford Street, York Way, 1903. This firm had a very large coal business as well as the builders and wheelwrights businesses in Rufford Street.

Cattle at Laycock's Dairy, c. 1830. Islington was a major source of London's milk supply in the eighteenth and nineteenth centuries. Cattle plague (1865) discouraged cow-keeping and led to stricter supervision. Conflict with the urban environment led eventually to the disappearance of the dairy farms.

Laycock's Dairy, Laycock Street, 1890s, with Laycock's Buildings (built in 1883) behind. Begun in about 1720, this was a large dairy farm between Upper Street and Liverpool Road. From the 1820s there were covered cattle pens, known as Laycock's Cattle Layers, used by drovers to rest animals overnight before going on to Smithfield Market.

The Old Barn, Laycock's Dairy, *c*. 1900. This photograph contrasts sharply with earlier views of the bustling dairy farm.

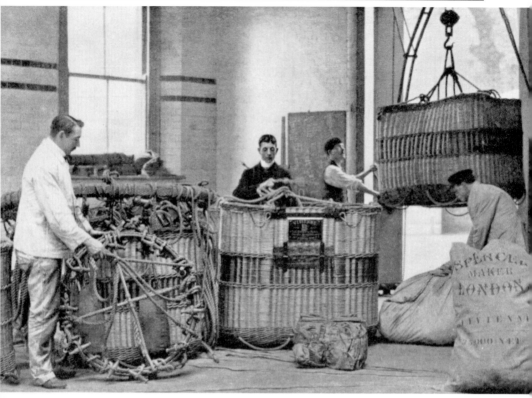

Spencer Bros., balloon factory, Highbury Grove, 1903. As well as being licencees of
Highbury Barn public house until 1957, the Spencers were pioneer aviators and
manufacturers. Herbert Spencer (d. 1949) claimed to be the first man to parachute from
a balloon, flown by his wife. Count F. von Zeppelin, the airship pioneer, is said to have
visited the balloon works.

ISLINGTON
AT PLAY

Mixed bathing at Hornsey Road Baths, c. 1924. The swimmer in the foreground is,

unaccountably, wearing spectacles.

Hornsey Road Baths, 1892.
The baths were designed by
A.H. Tiltman and opened by
the Lady Mayoress of
London on 26 July 1892.
The baths were bombed in
1941 and rebuilt in 1964.

Staff of Tibberton Square (Greenman Street) Baths, c. 1895. These baths were opened
27 April 1895 by Rt. Hon. Shaw-Lefevre MP, President of the Local Government
Board.

Mildmay Amateur Swimming Club, 1902. In the middle of the front row is Mr V. Jackson, President. Swimming was very popular at the turn of the century: by 1893 there were at least seven local clubs.

The official opening of Holford Square Bowling Green, 1935. During the Second World War the bowling green was used as a barrage balloon site; it was destroyed by a land-mine, along with much of the surrounding square.

North London Baths, Pentonville Road, *c.* 1865. Formerly known as the Pentonville Baths, the building dates from 1822–3 when it was opened by William Bragg. The provision of a bathing facility at this time was a piece of commercial opportunism, since the local bathing spas in Clerkenwell had all but disappeared, and the location of the new Pentonville Baths was located opposite the New River Company's reservoir in Claremont Square, from which it drew its water. The building survived until the early years of the twentieth century.

St John's Flower Show, Clerkenwell, 1899. From the anxious expressions of the children in this photograph, by local photographer H.W. Fincham, the judges' decision is imminent.

The gymnasium, Wharton Street, was founded in 1826 by Professor Voelker, a private teacher of gymnastics. At the time of its opening it was situated among the allotments of Myddelton Gardens. This site was chosen because 'it had the advantage of the purest air about London'. With the development of the Lloyd Baker Estate in the 1830s the area became what is currently Wharton Street. With the intention of reviving the knowledge and practice of gymnastics in England, Professor Voelker had formed the London Gymnastic Society, which grew to have 900 members and branches in Marylebone and Hackney. The Wharton Street Gymnasium could accommodate up to 300 gymnasts at one time. The utility of this institution was considered ideal for 'persons suffering from too unremitted study, or from excessive devotion to any sedentary pursuit'. It also provided great entertainment for onlookers.

Northampton Square bandstand and some very public entertainment for children in 1950. The bandstand still exists but Northampton Square today is more likely to echo with the sound of students from the expanded City University, which dominates one entire side of the square.

Northampton Square, 1950.

A cycling club outside Hudson's confectioner's shop, 1 Hazelville Road, Hornsey, *c.* 1909. Jack Moore is at the end of the row, on the left. Fourth from the right, in a stripey sweater, is his brother-in-law, Bert Davies.

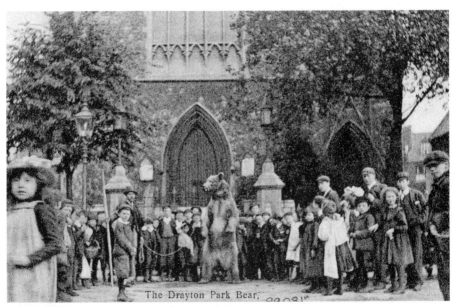

Dancing bear, Drayton Park, *c.* 1906. Italian street entertainers with dancing bears were still a common sight in Edwardian London. (Bear-baiting, a common sport locally, was forbidden by law in 1835.)

Cricket at White Conduit House, 1784. Cricket was played in the fields by White Conduit House in the eighteenth century. The White Conduit Club moved to Thomas Lord's cricket ground, Dorset Square, in 1787 and to Lord's Cricket Ground in 1814. White Conduit Gardens were built over the site in 1849.

Sunday school treat, starting out into Goswell Road with a good send-off from the neighbours, *c.* 1900.

The Marlborough Theatre, 397 Holloway Road, 1905. Designed by Frank Matcham, this building was opened as a theatre in 1903. The performance advertised here is by Mrs Patrick Campbell. The Marlborough began to show films in 1907 and was refurbished as a cinema in 1918. It closed in 1957 and was demolished in 1962. The site is now part of North London University.

Highbury Imperial Picture Theatre, 2 Holloway Road, 1926. The (silent) films showing are *Aloma of the South Seas*, starring Gilda Grey, and *Flame of the Yukon*. This cinema opened on 26 December 1912 and closed in 1959.

Section Eleven

CRADLE TO
CLASSROOM

*Fourteen sets of twins with their mothers under the care of the Child Welfare Centre,
League Street, off Old Street, 19 August 1929. Dr Booth, the Assistant Medical Officer of
Health, is on the right of the back row. The mothers are Mrs Murphy, Donnelly, Proctor,
Allen, Steckman, Blackellar, Marshall, Andrews, Pearson, Ashton, Clements, Longley,
Johnson and Abrahall.*

Marie Stopes (1880–1958), pioneer of birth control and sex education. She opened the Mothers' Clinic, 61 Marlborough Road, in 1921. Her most well-known book is *Married Love*.

The Mothers' Clinic, 61 Marlborough Road, *c.* 1924. Marie Stopes's clinic remained here from 1921 to 1925 and dispensed advice, help and contraceptives to mothers.

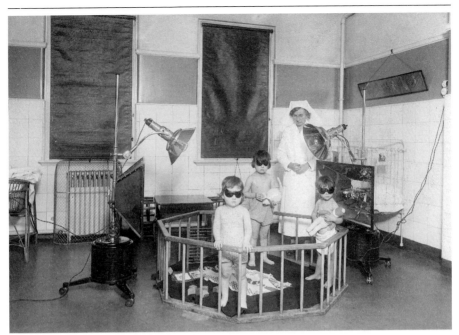

Pine Street Clinic, 1930s. A spell in the sun clinic, or 'can I go home now?'

Enjoying the fresh air on the roof of the League Street Maternity Centre, *c*. 1930.

The clinic for Italian mothers and babies, Pine Street, 1930.

The Monday morning clinic for Italian mothers and babies at Pine Street Maternity Centre, 1930. The clinic was run by Dr Booth, assisted by Mr Briondi.

Class 3A, Clerkenwell Parochial School, *c.* 1912. Founded in 1700 in Schoolhouse Yard, Aylesbury Street, the school moved to Jerusalem Passage in 1760. It finally settled in its present location, a purpose-built building in Amwell Street in 1830.

St Mary's Church School (Grove Street) infants, spring 1886, with Miss Hill, class teacher. The appearance of the children reflects the social problems of the area at this time.

Barnsbury Park School, 1906. This was a mixed Higher Grade School in Barnsbury Park, adjoining the LCC Housewifery Centre.

The arrival of the competitors at the Finsbury Horticultural Society's Flower Show held in Finsbury Town Hall, July 1938. There was no prize awarded to the scribbler who had misspelt 'flower show' in chalk on the pavement (left foreground).

AT YOUR SERVICE

Street-sweeping and watering machine, as supplied to Finsbury Borough Council by Karrier Motors Ltd of Huddersfield, 1933.

House refuse collection, 1933. The reorganization of street cleansing in 1933 in the Borough of Finsbury led to the replacement of the ten horse-drawn vans with three motorized vehicles. All streets were swept twice daily. The Wharf Road stables were closed and the horses and harnesses were sold. Two horse-drawn vehicles continued to be used for night rounds, but were hired for the purpose.

Inauguration of the Pluto Hot Water Lamp, 7 February 1899. Opened by Arthur Millward, Chairman of the Clerkenwell Vestry, on the corner of Exmouth Market and Rosebery Avenue, the Pluto Lamp not only served as a streetlamp, but also supplied a mug of tea, coffee, cocoa or a quart of hot water for a halfpenny; cold water was supplied free of charge. The lamp was similar to the one already operating successfully in Leicester Square. It proved to be an unsuccessful venture and was removed after six months at the expense of the Pluto Hot Water Syndicate.

New River Water Pipes, Goswell Road, *c.* 1905. Since 1613 the reservoir of the New River Head at what is today Rosebery Avenue had supplied the City of London with drinking water. The tree-trunks in Goswell Road are typical of the pencil-shaped, hollowed out trunks which conveyed New River water underground to streets and yards in the City. The narrow end of each trunk was inserted into the wide end of the next trunk and the joint secured with a belt and buckle. The interior of each hollow trunk was coated with lead to prevent rotting. Where water had to be diverted from the mains into buildings and yards it was achieved by using trunks with appropriately located branches; to these were attached quill-pipes, which lead into customers' homes. This system was in use for two hundred years until it was replaced with iron pipes.

Royal Northern Hospital, Holloway Road, 1905. The hospital was founded at Pembroke Villa, York Road, in 1856. It moved to Caledonian Road in 1864 and, as the Great Northern Central Hospital, to Holloway Road in 1888. It was opened by the Prince of Wales, later Edward VII, on 17 July 1888. The hospital was incorporated by Royal Charter in 1921 and known as the Royal Northern from 1924.

Domestic staff at the Royal Northern Hospital, 1912.

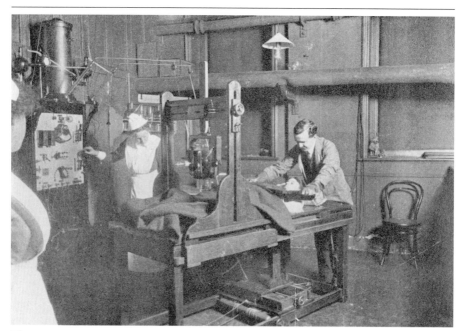

The X-ray Department, Royal Northern Hospital, 1911. This is in the early days of X-rays: the technology is very primitive.

The Royal Northern Hospital Outpatients Department, c. 1912. This was erected in 1888 and funded by a Ladies' Committee, presided over by Angela Burdett-Coutts.

Children's Ward No. 6 at the Royal Northern Hospital, 1911, with very starchy nurses, sister and doctor in attendance.

Lloyd Square, *c.* 1935. The lamplighter has arrived on his bicycle to extinguish the gaslight. He would return before nightfall to relight it. This practice continued into the late 1950s, when public gaslights were replaced with electrical equivalents.

The introduction of electric streetlighting, Goswell Road. In 1934 Finsbury Borough Council employed the County of London Electric Supply Company Ltd to replace existing gaslamps with electric streetlighting in all major thoroughfares in Finsbury. This decision was based on the comparison of gas and electrical lighting undertaken along Goswell Road.

Goswell Road, 1934.

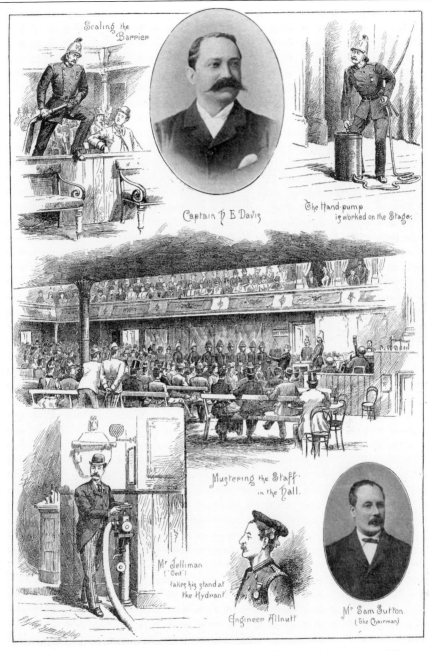

Scaling the Barrier

Captain H E Davis

The Hand-pump is worked on the Stage.

Mustering the Staff in the Hall.

Mr Jelliman ('Ted') takes his stand at the Hydrant

Engineer Allnutt

Mr Sam Sutton (The Chairman)

Fire drill at Deacon's Music Hall, 7 March 1891. The *Illustrated Sporting and Dramatic News* presents the incomparable Mr Sam Sutton's own fire-fighters, who emerge from the audience in full uniform and perform their fire-drill to his complete satisfaction and the reassurance of the patrons.

The stables at Islington Fire Station, *c.* 1910. This postcard was sent by Fireman Miller to his friend Miss Page, with the boast that 'we turn out in 25 seconds up here'.

Clerkenwell Fire Station, Rosebery Avenue, *c*. 1906. The station is the oldest operating fire station in Great Britain.

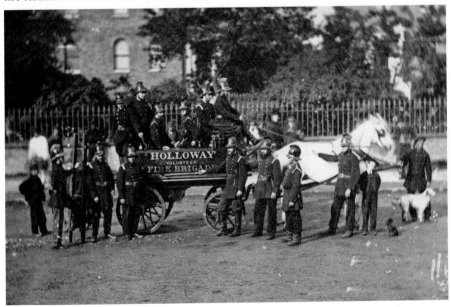

The Holloway Volunteer Fire Brigade, Seven Sisters Road, *c*. 1870. This brigade was formed on an entirely voluntary basis in about 1865. By March 1869 it had attended twenty-six fires. The station was in Seven Sisters Road near Crastin's Nursery. The brigade was still in action in 1870 but replaced in 1872 by the new Metropolitan Fire Brigade.

A turnout of the brigade at Islington Fire Station, 278 Upper Street, *c.* 1910. The station was built in 1899 by the LCC and was Islington's main fire station. Horse-drawn engines were in use up to 1921.

Clerkenwell Free Library, Skinner Street, 1967. The library was opened in 1890, with the innovative James Duff Brown as its librarian. By the time it was demolished in 1967, it was considered one of the most important libraries in Western Europe.

Clerkenwell Free Library, 1890–3. In keeping with other public libraries in the United Kingdom the library had operated with an indicator system and closed access. The public entered the reception area shown above and requested a book at the counter. This was produced from the storage shelves if the boards on the left 'indicated' its availability and location.

Clerkenwell Free Library, 1893–9. Open access to the bookshelves was first implemented in a public library at Clerkenwell in 1893. The public was free to browse and choose from the bookstock. In this building the 'supermarket' method was in use fully fifty years earlier than in the retailing business in Western Europe.

ISLINGTON AT WAR

'Islington's Own' Spitfire Mark V6, sponsored by the borough in 1941–2. The plane was sent to Gibraltar and used for training. It was damaged in a flying accident in 1942 and written off in February 1943.

Crowds look on as the Duke of Fife unveils the South African War Memorial, Highbury Fields, 15 July 1905. This memorial commemorates 110 men killed in the Boer War. The figure is entitled 'Glory' and is by the sculptor Sir Bertram McKennal, RA.

The South African War Memorial, Highbury Fields, *c*. 1924. This memorial commemorates 110 men killed in the Boer War. The figure is entitled 'Glory' and is by the sculptor Sir Bertram McKennal, RA.

Wounded servicemen at the Royal Northern Hospital temporary annexe, North Library, Manor Gardens, *c*. 1915. Some are young boys, but one or two others appear surprisingly elderly.

Christmas dinner for wounded troops at the Royal Northern Hospital, 1915.

The last wounded troops leaving the Royal Northern Hospital temporary annexe at North Library, Manor Gardens, in an impressive convoy of military ambulances, 31 March 1919.

Bomb damage from a Zeppelin raid, 144A King's Cross Road, 24 September 1917.

Bomb damage at St Mary's Islington, January 1941. The nave of St Mary's suffered a direct hit in September 1940, though the front part of the church, the tower and spire remained standing. The church was rebuilt and reconsecrated on 17 December 1956.

Bomb damage at an unidentified block, *c.* 1940. In the foreground is a street shelter. Many of Islington's worst bomb incidents involved direct hits on air-raid shelters, such as those at Annette Crescent and Eden Grove.

Finsbury ARP Fire Personnel during the Second World War. This photograph was provided by Mr T. Murphy (front row, third from the right).

Damage caused by a V2 rocket which fell in St John's Way at 5.15 p.m. on 5 November 1944.

Another long night's stay in a Finsbury air-raid shelter.

Entertainment in a Finsbury air-raid shelter during the Second World War.

Complete with paper hats, residents in Athelstane Road celebrate VE-Day, 1945.

Finsbury Labour Exchange, Penton Street. At the time the photograph was taken a mighty effort was in progress to encourage recruitment to the armed services.

UNDER LOCK AND KEY

On 11 May 1941 Pentonville Prison was severely damaged in an air raid, which demolished C Block and caused several fatalities.

Clerkenwell Explosion was the culmination of a year of Fenian activity in England. The Fenian Brotherhood was a militant group dedicated to the overthrow of English rule in Ireland. On 13 December 1867 an attempt was made to free Fenian prisoners held in the Clerkenwell House of Detention. The prison stood on the site of what is today Hugh Myddelton School, Sans Walk. While prisoners were expected to be exercising in the yard, an attempt was made to breach the outer wall in Corporation Row by detonating a barrel of explosive. The wall was breached and the terrace of buildings opposite was seriously damaged. Fifteen people died from injuries received in the explosion and forty were gravely injured.

The constables patrolling the neighbouring streets caught three people fleeing from the scene and later arrested others suspected of involvement, including Michael Barrett. At the ensuing trial, Barrett was convicted as the ringleader of the group involved in the explosion. Committed to Newgate Prison, he was executed on 26 May 1868, above the main gate of the prison, the last person to be executed in public in this country.

The House of Detention was closed in 1886, and the Hugh Myddelton School was built on the site and opened in 1893. Prison cells still exist underneath the school building and are accessible to the public.

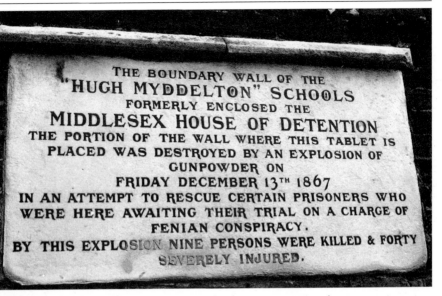

A plaque on the wall of Hugh Myddelton School commemorating the event.

The effects of the explosion in Corporation Row, Clerkenwell, December 1867. (Photograph by Bedford Lemere.)

The entrance to Coldbath Fields House of Correction, 1900. A few months later the building was demolished.

The treadwheel in Coldbath Fields House of Correction. Erected in 1794 the House of Correction soon gained a notoriety which earned it the description of 'the English Bastille'. Its exposed site, badly constructed drains and cruel regime contributed to a reputation of destroying both health and spirit in its inmates. Rioting inside and outside the prison had occurred in 1800 and 1830. This led to the introduction of the silent system, by which all communication by word, gesture or sign was prohibited. In the 1830s the treadwheel was also introduced; prisoners were required to walk on the treadwheel through 1,200 feet of ascent per day. The site of the House of Correction is now occupied by Mount Pleasant Post Office.

Holloway Prison, 1906, the year when the suffragettes were first imprisoned there. The old building was completed in 1852; the tower was copied from Warwick Castle. Originally a mixed prison, from 1902 it became women only. Demolition and rebuilding began in 1970.

Index